Our History
Lyrics 2010-2022

A Cast of Thousands
Edited by Beth Beer & Terry Cuddy

*This book is dedicated to Jim Andrews,
the original drummer extraordinaire,
who kept the beat going for 13 years.
We would've been lost without those chops.*

Record Records
Auburn, New York
Copyright © 2010, 2011, 2015, 2016, 2017, 2018, 2019, 2020, 2021, 2022, 2023, 2024 by A Cast of Thousands
All rights reserved

Names: Beer, Beth, 1972– editor.
         Cuddy, Terry, 1972– editor.
         Donovan, Thom, 1977–introduction.

Title: Our History: Lyrics 2010-2022 / A Cast of Thousands

Library of Congress Control Number: 2023919916
ISBN 979-8-218-21734-1

Designed and composed by Terry Cuddy

First Edition
Record Records 020

CONTENTS

Note on A Cast of Thousands ix

Acknowledgements xi

A Manifesto // A Cast of Thousands xii

Introduction // Thom Donovan xv

A Cast of Thousands
2010

Paranoia // Terry Cuddy 3
Another Day // Beth Beer & Terry Cuddy 4
Sunday Says // Donny Alger & Terry Cuddy. 5
Crazy // Beth Beer 6
(((GB))) // Beth Beer. 8
To Forget You // Marshall Stax. 10
Trust Lust // Terry Cuddy 12
Nowhere Fast // Beth Beer 13
Seasons Change // Terry Cuddy 15
The Drifter // John Reilly 16
Night Farming // Terry Cuddy 18
Bad Times // Beth Beer 19
Prayer // Donny Alger. 21
I've Been Leavin' Too Long // John Reilly 22

Aqua Fur
2011

Hot and Cool // Beth Beer 26
A Lullaby // Terry Cuddy. 28
Square Root (Radical Heart) // Terry Cuddy 29
Best Boy // Beth Beer & Terry Cuddy 30
Rumblings // Beth Beer 32
Superstition and Silence // Beth Beer & Terry Cuddy 34
Drop the Ax // Terry Cuddy 36
Tiny Pockets // Beth Beer 37
Hatful of Rain // Terry Cuddy 39
Neverman // Terry Cuddy 40
Let It Go // Beth Beer 41
Give Him Love // Beth Beer. 43
Fugitive // Terry Cuddy 45

Alone in the Crowd
2015

Vernacular Spectacular // Terry Cuddy & Taylor Price 48
In the Evening // Beth Beer 49
Wallace // Beth Beer 51
Ballad of Billy Blame // Terry Cuddy 53
Data Points // Beth Beer. 54
Salvation // Beth Beer 55
Razzle Dazzle // Terry Cuddy 57
Flaming June // Theresa Walsh. 59
R U Ready // Beth Beer 61
The Sound // Beth Beer 62
P.D.R.P. // Beth Beer. 64
We Bought a House // Beth Beer 66
It Shifts // Beth Beer. 68
Wonder // Beth Beer. 70
You Like // Beth Beer 72
Day Night // Beth Beer 73

The Fifth
2017

Our History // Beth Beer 76
A Stake // Beth Beer. 78
Way of Life // Terry Cuddy .81
Blinding Light // Beth Beer. 82
Big D // Terry Cuddy 84
Milestone // Beth Beer. 85
Andy Said // Beth Beer 86
From Within // Beth Beer. 88
Charade // Beth Beer 90
Judgment Day // Terry Cuddy 92
Resting Place // Beth Beer. 93
The Break Away // Terry Quill 95
Something // Beth Beer 96
Get Over // Beth Beer 97
Roundabout // Beth Beer 99
Bread and Circuses // Beth Beer 101

The BEIGE
2018

Gaslight // Beth Beer 106
Outlier // Beth Beer 108
Magical Thinking // Beth Beer & Terry Cuddy. 109
Adventurer // Terry Cuddy. 111
Cruel Will // Beth Beer 112
Around These Parts // Beth Beer. 114
Some Things // Terry Cuddy. 116
Shroud // Beth Beer 118
Regret // Terry Cuddy. 120
Savior // Beth Beer. 121

Sleeping World
2019

Big White Lie // Terry Cuddy. 126
Fantasy // Terry Cuddy 127
Collective Dementia // Beth Beer 128
Xmas in June // Terry Cuddy. 129
Numb the Fall // Beth Beer 130
Hot Summer Nights // Beth Beer 132
Blinders // Beth Beer 134
To Be a Woman // Beth Beer 135
Don't Forget // Terry Cuddy 137
Walkaway // Terry Cuddy. 139

Songs from the Second Floor
2022

No Detection // Terry Cuddy. 142
Decades // Beth Beer 144
Heading Nowhere Again //
    Rich Del Favero, Terry Quill, & d.b austin. 146
End the End // Terry Cuddy 147
It's Your Birthday // James Ruschak & Terry Cuddy. 148
Astrological Signs // Beth Beer. 150
Red Line // Beth Beer 152
Holiday in Amerika //Beth Beer & Terry Cuddy. 154
Hyper Individual // Beth Beer 155

Notes on A Cast of Thousands

A Cast of Thousands is a rock 'n' roll band from Auburn, New York. Beth and I started this band as a husband-and-wife duo after the break-up of our previous band Teenager. I named A Cast of Thousands after a bit from the Hollis Frampton film *Nostalgia*. The name is an inside joke rooted in avant garde cinema, where critique and art form are one and the same. My interest was to apply this concept to one of the most commercial art forms, rock 'n' roll. And "a cast of thousands" was the perfect name for such an unassuming endeavor.

Beth and I started out as the principal songwriters. We both sang vocals, while Beth played bass guitar and I strummed the six-string guitar. Along with Jim Andrews on the drums, we recorded our self-titled debut album in 2010. We then produced two more studio albums as a trio before asking, guitarist and long-time friend Terry Quill to join us in late 2015.

We continued to perform live gigs and record albums as a quartet, except during the height of the COVID-19 pandemic. Jim Andrews retired from the band in early 2023. Ryan O'Hara, the artist who designed most of our concert posters, joined on drums during the summer of 2023. Today we continue to perform and record in Central New York and the Finger Lakes region.

Our History: Lyrics 2010-2022 represents the lyrics from our first seven studio albums: *A Cast of Thousands, Aqua Fur, Alone in the Crowd, The Fifth, The BEIGE, Sleeping World*, and *Songs from the Second Floor*. The lyrics are in chronological order by year of album release and based on the track listing from each album. We hope you appreciate this new way to experience our music and know that we will have another studio album out in 2024 titled *You Can't Fight Spring*.

–Terry Cuddy
Fall 2023

Acknowledgements

We would like to acknowledge our fans who have kept us going for the past fourteen years. We would also like to give props to the music scene of Auburn, New York. The people who make up this community have fostered not only A Cast of Thousands but dozens of great musical acts and talented musicians over the last few decades.

We could not have produced our catalog or this book without the help of the artists, poets, writers, producers, engineers, and promoters who have offered their talents towards our mission. These collaborators include John Cuddy, John Beer, Eric Harvey, Taylor Price, Theresa Walsh, Donny Alger, Thom Donovan, Ryan O'Hara, Joe Librandi-Cowan, Jenny Chamberlain, Steve McAvoy, Blake Chamberlain, Laura Berman, Mirela Ivanciu, Kevin Dorsey, Joseph Scheer, Peer Bode, Andrew Deutsch, Charles Bernstein, Brandon Stosuy, Dave Gracon, Molly Jarboe, Lexie Howell, Emily Church, Steve Cerio, Chris & Anneke McEvoy, Chris Molloy, Chris Bauso, Phil Bauso, Damien Bauso, Amanda Franco, Mike Doyle, Mark Doyle, Andrew Roblee, Devon Roblee, Emily Powers, Rich Del Favero, d.b. austin, Marshall Stax, Greg Dopko, Lee de las Casas, Rick Basha, James Ruschak, Chris Reilly, Samantha Stepanski, Mike Parker, Rich Kegler, Patty & Roger Beer, Rachel Berrington Mike & Kathleen Cuddy, Dan, Mark & Matt Cuddy, Liam, Josh, & James Cuddy, Dorothea Cuddy, Patrick Kavanagh, Chad Latz, Peter Bakija, David Keay & Laura Feathers, Jack Rabid, Paul Silver, Jim Testa, Joe Wawrzyniak, Mark Suppanz, Matthew & Kerri Ross-McGuire, Jesse Conti, James Reichert, Juliette Zygarowicz, Ted Brill, Mike Burns, Duke Shanahan, Sandy Watson, Jeremy Johnston, Peter Krakow, Chris Ploss, Matthew Saccuccimorano, Alex Perialas, Andrew Giannettino, Amanda Rogers, Lynn Varley, Jenna Powers, Mark Feocco, Chuck Mason, Jimmy Giannettino, Ally Colvin and our family and friends who've been with us throughout the years.

We also must acknowledge the people who've influenced us and have passed on. These influences include John Reilly, Robert Lax, Ted Morgan, Tony Conrad, Colin Drayer, Paul Lyon, Margaret & Ray Cuddy, Teresa & Bill Foster, Marge & James Beer, Michael J. Cuddy, Sr., Nora Cuddy, Harald Bode, George F. Shatzel, Gil Jackson, and Nick Pennella.

A Manifesto

As we look back at pop music from the perspective of the early 21st century, we cannot help but nod to the past with some sense of loss. We do not want to confuse nostalgia with sentiment, but if we do, so be it. The pop music of the later half of the 20th century served its purpose. Any attempt to resuscitate it only dilutes its potent origin.

Now what used to be considered rock 'n' roll, resides in the margins of our culture. This is fine with us, for we are provincial. As capital awaits twilight, we can hear the codes return to sender. Rock 'n' roll can dream in its past again. We are witnesses, maybe participants. Without a leading role in this tragedy, we remain a cast of thousands.

INTRODUCTION
Mixing Pop and Politics

> *Mixing pop and politics he asks me what the use is*
> *I offer him embarrassment and my usual excuses.*
> —Billy Bragg

When Terry Cuddy and I first met as graduate students in Buffalo in the early 2000s we were mutually steeped in heady "avant-garde" art, poetry, and critical theory while on the side pursuing various extracurricular music projects. Although at the time these two realms felt totally discrete—a professor once scoffed when I mentioned improvising with a "noise band" in my spare time—of course nothing could be less true, both with regards to the past of popular music and its present (and I appreciate very much how this sentiment is articulated in A Cast of Thousand's *A Manifesto*). Rock and Roll, in particular, as a uniquely effective commercial vehicle for Pop in the post war, seems the place of overlap in the Venn diagram where mass appeal, innovation ("avant-gardism"), and socio-political content and messaging are integrated, as evidenced by countless groups, as well as in various contemporary artists' engagements with Rock music (for example, Dan Graham's documentary and accompanying book, *Rock My Religion*). It is this overlap, and its uses for our present, that is largely the focus of this introduction, though what I feel most compelled to do is reminisce and praise people who I have counted as my friends for the past two decades.

> *When bodies collapse,*
> *Decay is one reward*
> *For those of us left*
> *Guess what waits…another war*
>
> *As the future week conspires ahead*
> *The invisible fence we're up against.*
> *Sky is green, the sun turns red*

The alphabet is spinning backwards
A story to entertain us after
Headphones will ring
A bee will sing
To my wonderful darling

Outside my window, the wind is blowing colder
Only you can make the seasons change

Cause I was always dreamin'
Of the clear blue skies above us
And her eyes were the color
Of the solid earth below

I grow old
playing young
in my rock band

This is the moment
The moment I want to last
Last time I felt this
This way I sense its past

Signal out another turn
The absolute is never sure
Like the ache in my arm
It stays there and starves

    Listening to ACOT's catalogue and poring over their lyrics for the past months, I recall one of the central debates Terry and I engaged with in graduate school, which revolved around the intersection of politics and art. As you probably know, there is a longstanding debate about whether these two categories should be 'autonomous,' or whether they continuously animate one another, even, and perhaps even more so, when political 'content' would seem to be absent (what could be more political than the claim that one's work is not political?). During the course of these debates Terry and I both sided with the latter claim. Not only that, I think that our cohort of poets, filmmakers, video artists, and scholars at Buffalo and beyond dreamed of ways that art, politics, and life could become more seamless, perhaps looking back at international groups like Fluxus who also could not separate these categories. Why, for instance, are there not more poets who also act as politicians, as in the case of many indigenous societies historically, or in the discourse around international Negritude/Pan-Africanism, for just two extremely broad and variegated examples. While there have been poets who have assumed this role—Amiri Baraka's political leadership in Newark, NJ immediately comes to mind—they tend to be an exception within a US context, and this to me points to a problem with the political culture/system in general. Then again, maybe if we read 'poet' (or 'artist') more broadly we would find that musicians largely fill the vacuum once occupied by poets elsewhere. It is no accident, for instance, that Tupac was the nephew of one of the most radical of the Black Panthers, Assata Shakur; nor that Nina Simone's career suffered set-backs, to say the least, upon her assuming of a more explicit lyric of protest.

> *When you gain something you never wanted*
> *Well that's too bad*
> *When you lose nothing you never had*
> *Well that's just sad*
>
> *I may be dumb*
> *But I'm still pretty*
> *Tired of all this desire*
> *I don't feel anymore*
>
> *They sip their tea and wait in line*
> *To hear the prose of cops and criminals*
> *Ain't we so dandy,*
> *We look so fancy in drag*

Ain't we so dandy
We taste like candy in bed

Above the hills of chemicals
Rains down the new vernacular
Where "I" is "U" and "U" is "I"
And the whole is the particular

The now was quiet
The real was calm
It was united on all fronts
Excited by all fonts

the living the living
the dead the dead

The message is the stuff
The medium pulls it apart
And it collapses into dust
Guess it didn't mean that much

He showed me ones
I showed him zeros
Our love is cool
Like television

  How does the band become a place not only for comradery, collaboration, and friendship, but also a kind of platform that feeds back into other social and political actions and roles—say that of the journalist, in the case of Beth Beer Cuddy, or of a City Council member, in the case of Terry? What if the band was the place where, as Franco Berardi said during the Occupy movement in the early 2010's, a "social body" comes to be expressed through language (and song)? What is a fan when they are also a voter, or a potential ally in direct actions? How does the venue or rehearsal space become a place for informal political organizing? What if the work of the journalist could be done more effectively beyond print, on a stage, or in a video, or indeed through the publication of one's lyrics? I lament that I have not spent much time in Auburn, New York—the two occasions when I visited have been at the Cuddys' invitation—but when I walked the streets with Terry and Beth I was struck by their accountability; there didn't seem to be anyone they didn't at least have an acquaintance with, with whom there wasn't at least a glimmer of mutual recognition. What could be better evidence of community building, that which is at the core of a local (or as ACOT says, "provincial") political practice?

> *A photograph of my breakfast*
> *A contribution to our decline*
>
> *Oh my!*
> *It's quite the slump*
> *All the distractions*
> *Have given up*
>
> *a faith-based reality*
> *two thirds fever*
> *one third guile*
>
> *The stars in the sky*
> *have already died*
> *and still*
> *they are blinding us*
>
> *Life is short and that's no lie*
> *Don't waste time on an alibi*
>
> *"The world is all and that's the case"*
> *I read it once before*
> *If there's nothing more on this earth for me*
> *It's only you that I adore.*

this song's about hope
the real thing this time
the first i ever wrote
i find it sublime

So what are the lyrics saying (and we might ask just as easily, in the spirit of various theories of language, What are they doing?)? A lot of things that seem to have very little to do with politics obviously, and more to do with an ongoing meta-narrative of Rock and Roll and related genres: tales of messy break-ups and passionate love affairs; accounts of fugitives from the law, drifters, and outcasts; expressions of disdain for an adult world ignorant that a youth class prefigures the possibilities for other world building (it is no accident that the Cuddys' previous band was named Teenager); contempt for work as it precludes leisure, pleasure, and the fostering of intimate relationships. In addition to the themes and tropes that one finds in any Rock and Roll worth its salt however are songs that troll politicians and media pundits, not least of all Glenn Beck ("(((GB)))") and Donald Trump ("Savior"); songs that seem anthemic now of the critique of the financial and banking systems foregrounded by Occupy ("Around These Parts"); that address the United States' legacies of settler-colonialism and imperialism, as well as the ongoing anti-war movements which have opposed the US as a force of global military domination ("Another Day"); that also push back against the manner in which social media and algorithmic culture more broadly have captured a collective will and bent it to serve the inextricable projects of white supremacy ("Big White Lie"), gender-based oppression ("To Be a Woman"), and the extraction and enclosure of wealth ("Around These Parts"); that address a global climate crisis threatening the existence of life on the planet while augmenting existing injustices ("Decades," "Hot Summer Nights"). Songs like "Data Points" and "Salvation" highlight the alienation and isolation many of us feel in the wake of social media, particularly as it has exacerbated fascism in the most recent US political elections through censorship, disinformation, and the stoking of resentment. Beth's training as a journalist, as well as her position as a librarian, I can only speculate have made her uniquely aware of how social media has eroded an information commons.

It's like getting up
On a Monday morning
I take the sunlight
On my face as a warning

we forget our part in it all
we turn our backs on the past

we must choose how we live
we should choose not to die

Sometimes you have to shout aloud
For those who haven't figured out
How to stand up and to fight
For all the rights we had before.

we all crave a savior
we all crave a savior
someone who'll show us
the sun in his pocket

While I am providing this list of political subjects addressed by ACOT, something I fear may be lost in this introduction is an engagement with the beauty of ACOT's lyrics, and its aspirations as poetry, which as much as music is a place where Terry and I initially bonded. What would an effective political messaging be without beauty after all? As Wallace Stevens (the Wallace of "Wallace") says in his ars poetica, *Notes Toward a Supreme Fiction*, "It must give pleasure." To rectify this omission between the paragraphs of this introduction I have integrated some of my favorite lyrics. Maybe they are some of your favorites, too? If for some reason you have not also heard the songs they accompany, I realize how much can be lost between lyrics as they appear on the page vs. on an album track. Instrumentation as well as vocal phrasing and tonality add layers of meaning to lyrics obviously and vice versa. Yet another layer of meaning that I feel is important, but may be tedious to address in any exhaustive way is the question of (sub-)genre, the substance of much literary analysis. What I will say is this: that the choice of Rock and Rock sub-genres and adjacent genres (Country perhaps most of all) is also an important vehicle for meaning and what genre theorists used to like to call "intertextuality" (the way texts, songs for instance, are made up of other texts). As I listen to ACOT, considering genre—and perhaps this is just what all listening to pop music entails?—becomes a kind of game. *Oh, this is them doing Grunge, or Sonic Youth, or Willie Nelson, or Surf Rock, or Orange Juice,* etc. This is a particularly fun game to play with ACOT, where there is so much variety of musical styles and genres not only across albums, but within them. I wonder if Terry's expertise as a sound engineer (yet another hat that he wears is as a teacher of video and sound production to high school students) have not contributed to this aspect of ACOT's sound.

> *Never believe*
> *anyone who says*
> *he knows*
> *how to make it*
> *great again*
>
> *We shout into the void*
> *about things we've never read*
> *about things we've never seen*
> *We settle on a foe*
> *solid as evening fog*

so we don't have to deal
with what we've done

Christmas in June
I never meant to hurt you
I never meant to make you cry
The Dalai Lama is not worried

I walk the fields rest a bit
And huddle down in kinship
Take a hit for the home team
Just to hear the whole world sing

Oh, the iron in our blood
Comes from the stars
Serves to show
How connected we are

There is light in despair
There is joy in meaning
There are shrines to tear down
And some are worth keeping

Oh, the countdown's begun
Koalas on the run
Precious sands
In the barrel of a gun

Oh, tumbling dice!
Wouldn't it be nice
To give chance a chance
For our last dance

    I also wanted to say, on a personal note, how deeply affected I am by certain ACOT songs, particularly "Around These Parts." As an erstwhile singer-songwriter, covering this song alongside listening to ACOT's catalogue and studying the lyrics collected here, I came to appreciate it as a retroactive anthem of the Occupy moment, and more broadly, as an important song in a tradition of folk ballads committed to social change and economic justice. As I have learned revisiting singing this past year through a daily practice, to take songs into one's body—to memorize and render them—is a very different activity than simply listening to, or even simply singing along with a song. When I sing this song I feel an intimacy between the singer and the people they are speaking of, whom have been exploited for their labor power and lied to by a corrupt political culture. While the subgenre is spelled out (socially committed folk ballad), there is a soft touch here, and for me a very concise form of analysis around contemporary class antagonism in the US as it is mediated by technologies like algorithms and data mining. I believe that such a song, as all important pop songs do, crystallize an affect that is collective, shared by many. It is radical in that it gets at the root of the US's political woes: the mass capacity ("collective dementia") to forget the past ("We turn our backs on the past") and to place the blame and responsibility for addressing past mistakes through political engagement on someone else ("We forget our part in it all"). There are so many gems in ACOT's catalogue—in fact zeroing in has probably been my biggest challenge in composing this introduction. I wanted to end my piece with this one because it has moved me and made me remember many important lessons I learned from the Occupy era, but also because it may underlie much of what I value about the intersection of politics and art in ACOT's output. By "mixing pop and politics," to quote one of the best songwriters to ever do it, ACOT have provided us with songs that have documented in crucial ways the political terrain of the past decade, especially as it links Central New York/Finger Lakes Region to the larger country and the world. May there be many more songs from ACOT to make us think, and feel, and engage meaningfully with one another!

THOM DONOVAN

A Cast of Thousands
2010

PARANOIA

Are you my guardian angel
Or a member of the CIA?
Is your proximity earnest
Or the means to a wage?
I guess it won't take long, for sure
You feel like a shadow,
A presence I felt before

The shutter snaps a picture
I look outside my front door
Is this truth elixir
Or the drink that I just poured?
Soon enough I'll find out,
If some body is really there.
Better yet I just won't even care

You think I think too much?
Yeah, I think I think too much
Me thinks we think too much
About you, about you, about me

You're my guardian angel
You're the FBI
You're the secret service
You're the eye in the sky
You are my reflection
A virtual mirror
Please don't be afraid…
To sit next to me

ANOTHER DAY

When thoughts come to pass
Engaged inside your mind
Purged with some regrets
Left you more than you could find

So time to move on
Seal the box, put the gown away
For another day

Letters so brittle, lines old
Yet read so new
They disintegrate too
Falling just beyond your view

So time to move on
Pack your bags, play a different song
The one that goes on.

When bodies collapse,
Decay is one reward
For those of us left
Guess what waits…another war

So time to move on
Close the box, put the dress away
For another day

SUNDAY SAYS

Sunday says, Don't wake up just to read.
Gotta write it down, it's what you need.
To figure the whole week while you're weak in the knees
Standing dizzy upon your feet.

As you feel light in your head,
As the light hits your head.
Ooo - Sundays says, yeah Sunday says.

Sunday says, I can sit and watch you dream.
While I wait for coffee, I'll have some cream.
If there were three of me, we'd still be asleep
Counting clouds of floating sheep.

That fly over my bed
And the newspapers I've read.
Ooo - Sundays says, yeah Sunday says.

Oh, yeah! It's Monday's face they all dread
As the future week conspires ahead
The invisible fence we're up against.
Sky is green, the sun turns red.

Lightning striking again
To match my last cigarette.
Ooo - Sundays says, yeah Sunday says.

CRAZY

summer storm
electric air
worms in puddles

unfocused stare
can't keep track
of empty bottles

pastry box
whizzes by
collides with fingers

the mountain man
waving his arms
in anger

wires cross
nerve cells lost
we're all crazy

choosing you
like I did
exposed a sickness

how else
to explain
those years
and the time I wasted

no saner
then the man on the street
who gave me the finger

my head left me once
I think it's come back
much weaker

wires cross
nerve cells lost
we're all crazy

I'm no different

(((GB)))

Hey baby man!
Why you crying again?

Every time I turn on my TV
There's you blubbering, blubbering

About some nonsense
That never was
And never will be

Hey baby man
Why are you angry again?

Choking on chalk dust
Terrorizing us
End the lesson now

If you don't grow up
We won't show up
Or get down

Crybaby man
Crying like a crocodile
Crybaby man, crybaby man
Crying with the crocodiles
Crybaby man, crybaby man
Crying like the crocodiles
Lying man

You must be like me
So think for me

Sitting on your millions
Yeah, just like me, apparently

Face turning red
Tantrum brewing,
Ooh better watch out

You get ahead
Cuz you yell loud enough

So when you shut up
And we turn off
You'll be crying yourself to sleep
Wah-awah-wah-awah

Crybaby man
Crying like a crocodile
Crybaby man, crybaby man
Crying with the crocodiles
Crybaby man, crybaby man
Crying like a crocodile
Lying man.

TO FORGET YOU

People see me comin',
They always act dismayed
I guess I stayed when I should have left
And you left when you should have stayed
I don't see why my future has turned into my past
Let me thank you though one more time
You set me free at last
Now I have time for all the things
You said I'd never do

And tonight I promise I'll forget you.

I remember the day that we first met
It was at the county fair
You had on a dress of blue cotton
Red ribbons–in your hair
You said your name--it was Cara Finn
That was the first of many lies
But I didn't know it, at the time
I was arguing with your eyes
Those eyes like angel sapphires
From a dark bayou

And tonight I promise I'll forget you.

You said that I reminded you
Of your first real love affair
I wish you'd fill me in
A little more before I care
Now you say that your doin' better
You say it's a brand new day
Ahhh...people say all kinds of things

It's amazing what people will say
And meanwhile I stand here each afternoon
Staring at my shoes

And tonight I promise I'll forget you.

So these days I'm studying architecture
I build buildings in my head
I married Cheryl, she's a senator's girl
And I'm happy inside of her bed
But now and then she catches me
Staring into space
And I hate to see that disappointment
Written all over her face
'Cause I know she thinks the world of me
I know she's always true.

That's why tonight, I promise I'll forget you.

TRUST LUST

The voice of a whisperer says, "Hello, New York!
Wake that pretty head of yours."
In touch with all of your alter-egos
That means you can always quit.

The alphabet is spinning backwards
A story to entertain us after
Headphones will ring
A bee will sing
To my wonderful darling

I can't conquer lust
It sticks to the heart
Like truth to trust
Love must conquer lust
As it does, then we must be in love

Gamblers, cowards and picture takers
Sneak inside the dressing room
Offering up last minute instructions,
"The referee is to count to two"

The leisure suit from head-to-boot
Obscuring the cameras view
Believe me now, you must believe me
You can only see it when it's leaving

I can't conquer lust
It sticks to the heart
Like truth to trust
Love must conquer lust
As it does, then we must be in love

NOWHERE FAST

Stand still
My new life has just begun
It's bright
With all the stuff I've never done
It's coming fast
right up my throat
hope it lasts

The spot
Where I showed my pedigree
It's dry
from the blazing of my feet
A shooting star
straight to the bar
hope it lasts

Oh road!
Where do you go?
Nowhere fast

My mark
Made with disappearing ink
It shrinks
With all the wisdom that I speak
About my life
rolling on
hope it lasts

The time
speeds by without a pause
The lines
And gray show my flaws

The time is now
or never more
hope it lasts

Oh road!
Where do you go?

Oh road,
Nowhere fast

SEASONS CHANGE

Well, I didn't mean to bring you down,
but I just can't help it
It seems the weather's getting to me
Outside my window, the wind is blowing colder
Only you can make the seasons change

Winter snow may soothe the soul
On December mornings
As I hold you tightly in my arms
We danced before the fire as you took me higher
Than embers from the setting sun

Maybe it's the way the days are closing short
Maybe it's the way you breathe
Maybe it's everything you mean to me
Only you can make the seasons change

Spring came up so quickly
Well I really didn't notice
The flowers in your golden hair
I looked into your deep blue eyes and I felt an ocean
Only you can make the seasons change

Summer sun may promise fun to you my darling
As long as it is to you it is to me
No matter what I do or say, I just can't help it
Only you can make the seasons change

THE DRIFTER

I was headin' for Denver
Tryin' to change my luck
Everything that I owned I had
In a pickup truck
That's when I first saw her
In a small town café
Who'd ever thought I'd still
Be living here today

'Cause I was always dreamin'
Of the clear blue skies above us
And her eyes were the color
Of the solid earth below
And how we stayed together
Through all kinds of weather
I guess God only knows
'Cause I was a drifter
And she brought me home

I was a stranger
Just passin' through
And she was a hometown girl
That everyone knew
I was tired of driftin'
It's just another town
Had my head in the clouds
She was flat on the ground

'Cause I was always dreamin'
Of the clear blue skies above us
And her eyes were the color
Of the solid earth below

And how we stayed together
Through all kinds of weather
I guess God only knows
'Cause I was a drifter
And she brought me home

Just like a leaf that's caught
In a storm blown wind
Too many storms came through
So I could never begin
To find somebody
Yeah a girl like you
'Cause when you took my hand
That's when the sun broke through

'Cause I was always dreamin'
Of the clear blue skies above us
And her eyes were the color
Of the solid earth below
And how we stayed together
Through all kinds of weather
I guess God only knows
'Cause I was a drifter
And she brought me home
Oh I was a drifter
And she brought me home

A-ha-ha-ah-ah
Wo-ho-oh-ho-oh

NIGHT FARMING

Lights on the field
The crop I must yield
Brings me to your doorstep

I may be poor
caught under the gun
I need some understanding

Night farming
Night farming
Night farming

Call it research
As long as you stay
I call it vocation
If it keeps me sane

Around the corner
I cannot see
The silence follows
It's following me

Night farming
Night farming
Night farming

BAD TIMES

It's the time to
Give all that stuff away
Yeah-yeah
It's the time to do instead of say
Yeah yeah
We're all here to put on a big show
Yeah-yeah
This time near, no one can say no
Yeah-yeah

Stop all the mail
And cheer
We're gonna celebrate
Even bad times

All the monies gone
To the big old banks
Yeah-yeah
We sure know which guys we've got to thank
Yeah-yeah
Nothing left to give to you or me
Yeah-yeah
And all the work is done overseas

Turn off the phone
And say
We're gonna celebrate
Even bad times

Folks just finally coming awake
Yeah-yeah
To all the life that's at stake

Yeah-yeah
No more "So?"
No more millionaires
Yeah-yeah
No more noise
Clogging up the air

Get offline
And see
We're gonna celebrate
Even bad times.
Go outside just be
You and me
Here in bad times

PRAYER

Sexually humorous situations
Got perversions of every kind
They're required to weigh like
Broken box springs
Sprung from and on my mind

I need this to keep me laughing
'Cuz if I stop now I start crying every time
Somewhere I know the sun is shining
If it's not here for now
We'll paint it outside the lines

Please carry this prayer as a reminder
Of God's love for you and all of us who care
I hope you will ask God to help you
To do what you've gotta do
To get well again

Use your unique talent
To always help humanity
This will give your life a purpose
And help you break free
From the prison inside yourself

Please carry this prayer as a reminder
Of God's love for you and all of us who care
I hope you will ask God to help you
To do what you've gotta do
To get well again

I'VE BEEN LEAVING TOO LONG

I never knew if this day was coming
It seemed as though somehow it would go on and on
But I can tell that tonite's gonna be a hard one
'Cause I'm always hopin' for one last song

'Cause I've been leavin' too long
I wish that I could sing just one more song
But it's too sad – though sad isn't wrong
It's just that I've been leavin'
I've been leavin' too long

I can't pretend I can't pretend any longer
That things are going the way you want them to
I wish I could 'cause, honey, I want to please you
But it's too much, it's too much for me to do

'Cause I've been leavin' too long
I wish that I could sing just one more song
But it's too late – the time is all gone
It's just that I've been leavin'
I've been leavin' too long

Aqua Fur
2011

HOT AND COOL

In the mass age
a screen, a scream
between

Content formed
feasting eyes
never the wiser

Flat and broke
a vacant stare
past the yard line

It goes south
furious
quite the ending

You're a record
spinning tape
a relic

Broken lightbulb
the dark
more than enough

We play ping pong
in a courtyard
slick and icy

Things go south
delirium
in the meantime

Catch the cast
sleazy mark
brutal bedlam

Pinpoint dots
strain the eye
yawn of boredom

I grow old
playing young
in my rock band

It goes south
curious
till the next frame

A LULLABY

This is the moment
The moment I want to last
Last time I felt this
This way I sense its past

Ooo!

Past the present's future
Future tense unto me
Unto me visions, euphoria, ecstasy

Ooo!

I hold you so gently
So gently I hear you breathe
Breathe in so deeply
So deep inside your sleep

Ooo!

There is nothing
Nothing more that I could give.
I give all the love I have
To you kid.

Ooo!

√♥

The square root of my heart
Is twice as much as his
And one tenth of yours.
I'm losing space and time

Keep it on your calculator
I can't complete the computation
The square root of my heart
I don't know where to start

Heard about the architecture
I don't need to hear another lecture

Even if it's scarred
Keep it on the clock
Beat it 'til it stops
The ticking in your car

Signal out another turn
The absolute is never sure
Like the ache in my arm
It stays there and starves

Read about the resurrection
A one way ticket to teenage heaven

BEST BOY

it must be some kind of gift
to always be right
secure inside your authority
faking science to hide truth from reality
now it shows
it shows, it shows, it shows
it shows, it shows, it shows
who's bought and sold

when years of experience
breed words of indifference
something's missing
numbers are cooked
bribes overlooked
all strings attached
and it shows
it shows, it shows, it shows
it shows, it shows, it shows
who's bought and sold

you're on the inside now
deeper than you ever thought
what once was an empty well
now it's filling up
so swim, and swim,
or else you are sunk
just like us
so it goes

it shows, it shows, it shows
it shows, it shows, it shows
who's bought and sold
it shows, it shows, it shows
it shows, it shows, it shows
we're bought and sold

RUMBLINGS

The silver spoon
just out of reach
The classic line
is somewhat weak
The phone,
it rings and rings
and rings
A quarter tone
a pounce, a squeeze

I'm impressed
by your shop
of hype
Sell me something
and I'll bite, I'll bite
I'll buy the web
the script, the type
And you'll watch
as it all falls down,
falls down

Treble, tremor
the ground is shaking
feel the Earth
Hear the rumbling

Treble, tremor
the ground is shaking
There's no time
Hear the rumbling

The Other
is here to stay
No matter what
laws you make, you make
The seismic shift
is long overdue
And you have
lost your clue

I salute
your lack of soul
That's a joke
if you don't know, don't know
You make a scratch in a
totaled car
That's how relevant
you are

Treble, tremor
the ground is shaking
feel the Earth
Hear the rumbling

Treble, tremor
the ground is shaking
There's no time
Hear the rumbling

SUPERSTITION AND SILENCE

Silence
You're my kind of silence
The kind that don't get me down
When I'm out on my own

Violence
Superstition and violence
The kind that I watch on TV
When I'm all alone

Patience
Passing through it timeless
I've got too much on my mind
Makes it hard to forget

Prudence
It's not like it you used to be
Perhaps you should stay
Stay away

Don't you know that everything
Will be all right

Kindness
Someone give me some notice
Just a glance if you can spare
It would make my day

Vicious
Sort of like sadistic
Sneak a peek without
Anybody else aware

Ponder
If you will this life
I know I don't matter
But act like you care

Silence
You're my kind of silence
The kind that don't get me down
When I'm on my own

Don't you know that everything
Will be all right

Salvage
Just take what matters
Leave the rest behind
We don't want it no more

DROP THE AX

How come it took so long for you to drop the ax
That chopped my heart in two
And when the bell has rung, behind the smoking gun
Your smile was slightly cruel

I always knew when you were lying
'Cause I could hear you laugh when you were crying
But yesterday topped it all, when you said, "Goodbye."

Now in the aftermath, an alcoholic crash
That split my brain in half
Now my voice is gone, it's cracking like the sun.
So I don't talk to no one

Beer after beer I did drink
To my ex who played me like a puppeteer
'til one day she cut the strings, with my own shears

'Though I always knew when you were lying
'Cause I could hear you laugh when you were crying
But yesterday topped it all, when you said, "Goodbye."

TINY POCKETS

Where is my brain?
Over in a lake
Tangled up in algae
Trying to buy a break

In the air, a massive change
Something here not the same

I'm still go lucky
More highs than lows
Shirt thrown on backwards
Got miles to go

Till he's eating endless teething
Heart socket, tiny pocket

And it drives me on and it burns me so
Love forever, love unknown
And it drives me on, and it drives me around
And it burns my soul
Oh-oh
Oh-oh-oh

I'm masquerading
Try it on for size
It fits so smoothly
Kind of like a lie

Piggies, rings under eyes
Where's my body?
Where are my thighs?

Here comes the spider
Wheels on a bus
Man's dog is BINGO
What is *Trust Lust?*

Smile sweet, heart full
Love him so, got to know

And it drives me on and it burns me so
Love forever, love unknown
And it drives me on, and it drives me around
And it burns my soul
Oh-oh
Oh-oh-oh

HATFUL OF RAIN

Caught up in the race
Got a steady place
To keep your feet on the ground

Woke up in a town
With no friend around
To hang your head on this time

And it seems you got stuck with
A hatful of rain

You read down the page
You better save face
Before they take you away

It's a movie scene
Someone else's dream
That keeps you awake

And it seems you got stuck with
A hatful of rain

When you gain something you never wanted
Well that's too bad
When you lose nothing you never had
Well that's just sad

NEVERMAN

I never change the channel
At least not anymore
I never take a chance
Or settle scores

I never fold the corners
Or leave marks on the page
Never left the planet
In words there's outer space

I am the Neverman
In Neverland, so nevermind

I never mailed a letter
Or wrote a note
I never crossed Niagara
By bridge or boat

Never felt so tired
I think I'll go to bed
Never look out my window
I think that's what I read.

I am the Neverman
In Neverland, so nevermind.

LET IT GO

The match to ignite
A spark in my head
You blew it

Tossing away
A knotted thread
Of your choosing

A silent dance
A nod of ascent
Is all it took

To focus on this
Regiment
And not what it should

Can you feel this
Can you feel this
Can you feel this
Can you feel this

I am nothing to you
Just looking at you
Makes me tired

I lost this chance
My pride intact
A moment's notice

I am nothing to you
I am nothing to you
I am nothing to you

I am nothing to you
I am nothing to you
I am nothing to you

Can you feel this
Can you feel this
Can you feel this
Can you feel this

It's like a prickling you can't deny
Just let yourself go
Let it go

You are not me
I am not you
It's a blessing

I will move on
I will march on
Without you

Wouldn't it be
Wouldn't it be
Wouldn't it be

How dare you still have power over me

Can you feel this
Can you feel this
Can you feel this

It's like a prickling you can't deny
Just let yourself go
Let it go

GIVE HIM LOVE

Blinders on
Get ready to drive
Sweetly singing
To you, you, you

I never know what lie
I will find
You complete me
You reduce me

So here we go and here we go
It's my turn now just so you know
So hang on tight, it's bumpy as hell
He's gonna cry, get ready now

Give him love
From me
Give him love, give him love
From me

I'm a child
In a grown up body
I'm mild and mighty peculiar
I don't see
What you see in him

Do you think it would be better
To look there…
Or elsewhere
To find what
You're searching for

I may be dumb
But I'm still pretty
Tired of all this desire
I don't feel anymore

So give him love
From me
Give him love, give him love
From me
Give him love, give him love,
Give him love from me
Give him love, give him love
From me

It's a close up
Of your ambition
A time lapse
An ancient secret
It's pointless
It clearly is

Here's my road map
To take us nowhere
A bear trap
That catches nothing
We don't need anyway

So throw it, throw it
Throw it all away
Hesitant but do it today
Sorry spin
Sorry

Give him love from me

FUGITIVE

Big freight train take me away
From the city lights to the borderline
The faster you go the further I'll be
In two days time

They'll be huntin' for me miles around
70 road blocks from my hometown
The further you get the freer I'll feel
In two days time

I'm a fugitive on the run from the law
Stole some money
Then something went wrong

$70,000 in cold hard cash
Got one bullet, but no gun to match
If I jump off now, they'll find me soon
If I wait too long, gonna meet my doom

I'm a fugitive on the run from the law
Stole some money
Then something went wrong

The hole in my chest is bleedin' bad
If I don't wake up tomorrow you can keep the cash
Big freight train - keep on movin' fast
Big freight train - keep on movin' fast

I'm a fugitive on the run from the law
Stole some money
Then something went wrong

Alone in the Crowd
2015

VERNACULAR SPECTACULAR

Beneath the clouds the city sky
Sheds light on all of its ambassadors
They sip their tea and wait in line
To hear the prose of cops and criminals
Ain't we so dandy,
We look so fancy in drag

In the morning on the tips of tongues
They chant the word *'abstantia'*
They sow the seeds that never grow
In the minds of minute militia
Ain't we so dandy
We taste like candy in bed

Above the hills of chemicals
Rains down the new vernacular
Where "I" is "U" and "U" is "I"
And the whole is the particular
Can you see the writing?
Can you hear the writing bounce off the wall?

Can you hear the writing on the wall?
Can you hear the writing on the wall?
Can you hear the writing on the wall?
Can you hear the writing on the wall?

IN THE EVENING

End the race
Our final embrace
Fallen through the looking glass
Our time is still marching

Brown turns to gray
Silent today
Closing of the curtains
The clock is just slowing

And I feel
Down, down
Down, down
When you're not around
Around, around
In the evening

Time speeds fast
Youth miscast
A moment in the summer
Turns into winter

And I feel
Down, down
Down, down
When you're not around
Around, around
In the evening

A wrinkled place
Constricts your face

I watch as you slip away
You'll always be with me

And I feel
Down, down
Down, down
When you're not around
Around, around
In the evening
In the evening
In the evening
In the evening

WALLACE

The world was quiet
The house was calm
No flicker came from the TV
Silence stretched on sweetly
Divine
Wanna try sometime?

The hot was quiet
The word was calm
It fluttered open like a look
Sentence structure hook
It's wide
Wanna step inside?

The work was quiet
The horn was calm
The tempo pulsed upon the page
Electrified the brain
A spark
To ignite the heart

The heart was quiet
The worth was calm
The marks and lines and shapes adorn
Truer meaning forms
A light
Fuels a summer night

The world was quiet
The house was calm
The landscape soared across the way
Taken to some place

Away
From the somber day

The now was quiet
The real was calm
It was united on all fronts
Excited by all fonts
Surprise
Life before your eyes

THE BALLAD OF BILLY BLAME

Look away in a distant gaze
A magic mark on a paper plate
Some pretty words, soup of decay
A public nuisance, there is no escape

This is a story of fisticuffs
No one to lick, no one to touch
You think, you think, you think too much
In this world, there is nonesuch

This is an echo, a fallen wall
No time to write, no time to call
A radio face, a lazy eye
So macho, yet so shy

This is the story of Billy Blame
Pointing a finger, naming a name
A game show host without a game
Is there no pride? Is there no shame?

A live broadcast, a parking garage
Was that a sign, or a mirage?
Epic soundtrack, any montage
Just something to throw into the–bin

This is the tale of a dittohead
Can't remember just what he said
One more jerk–off to bed

The living the living
The dead the dead

DATA POINTS

Our tools they reshape us
I screened you inside my heart
And I looked into your eyes once
Didn't think I saw that much

The message is the stuff
The medium pulls it apart
And it collapses into dust
Guess it didn't mean that much

But I love you so much
And our love feels so true
You're my everything
Love extreme
You're my destiny

Our time it reshapes us
Ticking down to some place new
And it measures out into a pulse
It flows and ebbs on cue

The signals they track us
Points of data lined up like stars
And they're guiding over to a loss
Tied together but so far.

But I love you so much
And our love feels so true
You're my everything
Love extreme
You're my destiny

SALVATION

I bought a halo
On the Internet
It was cheaper
Than e-cigarettes
It came from China
With a manual
Full of sirens
And benzene

I found religion
On the Internet
It was shiny
Taste of spearmint
It made me whole
It made me so full
Until I got
The big bill

Oh how, oh how
Did it get so far
Oh how
Oh how
We are
Who we are

Next page

I met my boyfriend
On the internet
He said he never
Felt like this

He showed me ones
I showed him zeros
Our love is cool
Like television

I made myself
On the Internet
I mixed Twitter
With some Instagram
I look so tall
I look so tall
Unreal
That's the best of all

Oh how, oh how
Did it get so far
Oh how
Oh how
We are
Who we are

RAZZLE DAZZLE

Razzle dazzle
Give me something
I can't handle

Jeepers creepers
Tag my toe
To see how much I care

I'm not alone
When it comes to this
I think I've been before

I'm not as sick
As I want to be
Come on and
Gimme some more

Don't get down
Don't get me down
Everything will be all right
And even if you were wrong
You could say I was right

Stretch your way
Out of a plastic bag
Stick around for awhile
Wait in front of a mirror
Until you see a smile

You're not alone
When you clench your fist
Hatred has its funny ways

The clock strikes
Quarter to six
Begin to count the days

Don't get down
Don't get me down
Everything will be all right
And even if I was wrong
I could say you were right.

I was right
You were right
I was right
You were...

Right

FLAMING JUNE

Alone again she's crying
Her lullaby to sleep
Dreaming of a family
A love she'd ever keep

While she lies there sleeping
They watch the setting sun
All the lovers on the beach
She has no one

Love can't come too soon
For Flaming June

Mama died when she was born
Daddy didn't stay
Taken in by strangers
Not loved one day

She didn't turn to pills
She didn't turn to drink
She just turned inside herself
Living on the brink

Love can't come too soon
For Flaming June

While she lies there sleeping
The horizons all a glow
The artist sees her beauty
Will she ever know

While they lie there sleeping
Behind them sets the sun
Her and her artist
She is a now a loved one
She is a now a loved one
She is a now a loved one

R U READY

These incidental marks of progress
The tally sheet is what keeps us in line
A photograph of my breakfast
A contribution to our decline

R U ready
U ready for the change
Oh it's headed your way

Stacks of cash thrown into the wind
The blaming game has just started
Pretty words shouted over the din
Dismantling the last bastion

R U ready
U ready for the change
Oh it's headed your way,
It's headed your way
Oh it's headed your way
It's headed your way

I like you do you like me
Never mind we'll never meet
Skeletons hang in the breeze
They dance and sway whole world can see

R U ready
U ready for the change
Oh it's headed your way
It's headed your way
Oh it's headed your way
It's headed your way

THE SOUND

Oh boy!
The frogs are gone
They packed a suitcase
They're moving on
And we're next
It's in the stars
No one lasts
Very long

Oh well!
It's been fun
With all the shouting
That's going down
It's all smoke
A reddish fish
Lights out
Make a wish

The sound
It drowns
The sun
It pounds
It pounds
We'll dance
And sing till the end

Oh my!
It's quite the slump
All the distractions
Have given up

Now it's real
Without its screen
It's all bare
Nothing to see

So now
We take our bow
With no one clapping
It's nice somehow
It's all good
A little break
A rest
From mistakes

The sound
The sound
The sound
The sound
The sound

It drowns
The sun
It pounds
It pounds
We'll dance
And sing till the end

P.D.R.P.

The stars are shot tonight
Cloud covers the light
You sell your soul for fame
You lost your mind

Nothing's ever made for free
So much is dried up
Better deal down the street
Just have to put out

The P.D.R.P. is calling again
To set your life
The P.D.R.P. is calling you again
To correct your life
The P.D.R.P. is calling you again
To snuff your life
The P.D.R.P. is calling you again
They're right

Your dreams are made of strings
Break at the slight
This is all you'll ever be
Trapped in twilight

This is the fix for you
For only $9.95
Gonna create a perfect suit
Just a little tight

The P.D.R.P. is calling again
To set your life
The P.D.R.P. is calling you again
To correct your life
The P.D.R.P. is calling you again
To snuff your life
The P.D.R.P. is calling you again
They're right

WE BOUGHT A HOUSE

We bought a house
Filled it with stuff
Top of a hill
Feeling something

We dreamed the dream
Upon a time once
Brown-covered snow
Push down the street

That was now
This is then
That was now
This is then

Our turn at bat
Ink on the line
To sell is the best
If you can get offers

No you; only me
Number is one
Strong survive
On weakened shoulders

That was now
This is then
That was now
This is then

It started slow
Green turned to red

Nothing can stand
The bridge is falling

Poor fighting for
Rich men's dreams
So they collect
The prize, the lie

That was now
This is then
That was now
This is then

IT SHIFTS

Where do we belong
took this quiz and I found
my place is right beside you
no test could be wrong
what kind of person could I be
Beyoncé or Carrie
it's not the name defines you
give a roar or be brave

And it shifts
it tilts
it grows
neverless

What higher power could there be
Apple or TV
I'm thinking different darling
then we're all the same
What object am I most like?
a sandwich or that bike?
I need to classify it
then I'll crush it down

And it shifts
it tilts
it peaks,
neverless

tunes all sound the same
made in an arcade
we have it all and nothing
all and nothing more

And it shifts
it tilts
it's gone,
neverless

We have all and nothing
all and nothing more
We have all and nothing
all and nothing more

WONDER

I've felt old since I turned 26
I feel so tired since I notice less
I am nothing that you ever miss
Like a newspaper caught in a snowdrift

I wonder
I wonder
Why I feel so small
I wonder
I wonder

I've been here before heard the same exchange
Another round, waste your bottle of beer
Nothing's changed
Another coin in the jukebox, baby
Numb your pain
You go where you need to go
Go insane

I wonder
I wonder
Why I won't do much
I wonder
I wonder

Here I am nearly 43
Nothing to my name
Stumble past opportunities,
Make you blush with shame
I give up before you can give up on me
I just want to be left without anything
I wonder

I wonder
Why I'm here today
I wonder
I wonder

YOU LIKE

You like to hide, you like to hide, you like to hide
You like to lie, you like to lie, you like to lie
Dregs of pride, dregs of pride, dregs of pride

You have your passions
And believe in all that you do
You click away in your cave,
A true hero in blue

You like

You like to hide, you like to hide, you like to hide
You like to lie, you like to lie, you like to lie
Let's all high five, let's all high five, let's all high five

You set the record straight
Gnarled and scratched to distort
Cognitive dissonance
Is your favorite sport

You like

DAY NIGHT

Day night
Night day
A break before the next line

Pilot
No breaks
Crashing headfirst into white

Irate
Open flame
Burning everything in sight

Slow down
Long wait
We'll wait until it fades away...it fades away

Tail light
Busted
No cop around to make it right

Sold out
Courage
A straw man setting up to fight

Bluster
Flustered
Red balloon set to pop

Slow down
Long wait
We'll wait until it fades away...it fades away

The Fifth
2017

OUR HISTORY

Our history
is broken in pieces

there is no right,
but plenty of wrong

we dish it out,
yet we can't take it

the fury
the raging sound

a mishmash
of flags and men

alcohol
fuels all the lies

we linger
for keeps
we call that discovery

a masquerade of actors
change the course
invent the tale

a faith-based reality
two-thirds fever
one-third guile

we sing the songs
of olden times

we dream the dreams
already died

we proudly preen
our greatness

an oily sheen
of artifice

we battle on
blindly

frozen solid
in line

A STAKE

pushed to the limit
of mindless distraction
i crumble at my feet

nobody's watching
as they take apart
the concrete on main street

destroy till it's broken
the masters arrive
sweep up the crumbs that are left

praise to the leaders
hand over the keys
then you can't say it's theft

time to clear your throat
let the words give a sting
to those who do you harm
time to amp up the noise
there's a whole lot of us

stake
and claim
away

tune out the masses
and build up the messes
the middle starts to shrink

hope is a feather
assembled in china
the quill has no ink

years of blindness
fueled tacit approval
we slumbered easily

dangle the carrot
then hit by the stick
no rest for the weary

time to clear your throat
let the words give a sting
to those who do you harm
time to amp up the noise
there's a whole lot of us

stake
and claim
away

build the oasis
propped up by deceit
the storm engulfs us all

batten down hatches
call up the guard
put up a paper wall

noise and static
clog up the drain
our frantic theme song

we are your data
to use as your pawn
and now let's all sing along

time to clear your throat
let the words give a sting
to those who do you harm
time to amp up the noise
there's a whole lot of us

stake
and claim
away

WAY OF LIFE

I open the seal to reveal
Every secret I've concealed
Now I'm at wit's end
And I can no longer pretend

This way of life I'm livin'
All take and nothing given
And it's an empty plane
No passenger remains

I closed my little red book
It was blank every time I looked
I'm not lookin' for sympathy
'Cause it's the last thing you'll get from me

This kind of life I'm leadin'
If it's convenient, I believe it.
And it's the empty space
Where innocence wants to stay

I taste the apple you gave me
Once was blind, but now I can see
This sin was not your own
It was mine and mine alone

This kind of lie I'm leadin'
I'm a man, I'm all-deceivin'
And I've destroyed this land
I've turned the garden into sand.

BLINDING LIGHT

I'm at a loss
to describe it
but it feels like
a vise tightening

Lost in a land
of nightmares
for I can't tell
what I'm seeing

The man in the moon
is laughing at us
because we are ridiculous

Claw around for
some ground
you continue
to deceive me

Stand on top
of piles
of dirty lies
what are you thinking

The stars in the sky
have already died
and still
they are blinding us

Full of disgust
I turn off
all the screens
around me

Wanting to feel
something real
electrical
a pulse inside

The central force
is not ourselves
it is, and must be Love

BIG D

Big D has got all the answers
Even though you don't wanna hear them
Even though she doesn't wanna hear this song
Because it's about her, and it might be true

Big D has all the bases
Covered up down in the basement
Even though she's never gonna use anything
That she's kept away from you and from me

Because she's always lived her life
The way she wants us to live our lives
Make a choice and stick with it,
Don't show your cards, don't fold too quick.

Big D is such a force of nature
To reckon with from the beginning
All the way to the ninth inning
So she won't miss a second of play

Big D is the only one who
Knows the ones who knows the ones who
Get things done the way she wants them to
That way we know just what to do

Because she's always taught us all
To be ourselves and stand up tall
Make a mark and make it stick
Don't second-guess, don't ever quit.

Big D has got all the answers
Even though you don't wanna hear them
Even though she doesn't wanna hear this song
Because it's about her, and it might be true

MILESTONE

Another milestone
crushed to dust
Another dream
coated in rust

Can it be
that my life is half over
My May
has turned into October
And it's etched in my face
the cracks come at rapid pace

A class reunion
to ignore
A smaller life
to explore

I count on one hand
what I've accomplished
It fails to outnumber
what I promised
And I'll get it right
I'll get back on that bike

ANDY SAID

strike a pose
like Andy said
it's always fleeting
better than dead
the brand of winners

figure out
who you've become
your Instagram
has lost its lure
but keep it rolling

this oversharing
of your life
leads to more
obscurity
so give up the game

in this instant snapshot
of hollowness
celebrity
no gift is recognized

left alone
disturbing thoughts
pick up your phone
ignore the corporation
recording them

they'll take the pieces
depend on most
won't matter that

you can't pay the costs
of soul invasion

this oversharing
of your life
leads to more
obscurity
so give up the game

in this instant snapshot
of hollowness
celebrity
no gift is recognized

FROM WITHIN

the riot gear
is handed out
the color fear

emotions high
warming up
the atmosphere

the time
the time
for crossing lines

It always was
tenuous
at best

the fever hot
bringing with it
pestilence

the time
the time
for breaking lives

destruction
comes from
within
destruction
comes from
within
destruction
comes at a whim
It comes from within

the danger real
a force
of reckoning

based on a lie
spewed forth
by false kings

the time
the time
for choosing sides

the rule of law
crushed out
by passion

violent turns
removes
compassion

the time
the time
to say goodbye

destruction
comes from
within
destruction
comes from
within
destruction
comes at a whim
It comes from within

CHARADE

you walk
then you stumble
your choice
one big fumble
you close your eyes
wait for something great
a dream
that's never coming

you sing
a song of hope
you slip
off that rope
you try to break
the habits of liars
a debt
of hooks and wires

And then you try to be
something marvelous
something beyond
anything

you sit
in your La-Z-Boy
you count
times of joy
and on your fingers
you slip
and you wonder
is this all it's for

you gaze
out the window
and think
of endless snow
piling on you
and making you bigger
all the ways
than you are.

JUDGMENT DAY

I don't care if it's Judgment Day
And I don't care if things are going my way

Except you, you're looking like you don't want to
So self aware in your own costume

And I catch you looking to see
Watching me act so care free,
Take my hand and we can be.

Life is short and that's no lie
Don't waste time on an alibi
Youth isn't something that you just go buy
The present is always at our side

If you tell me what to do
I will try to make it true
One and one and one is two

"The world is all and that's the case"
I read it once before
If there is nothing more on this earth for me
It's only you that I adore.

And I catch you looking to see
Watching me act so care free,
Take my hand and we can be.

If you tell me what to do
I will try to make it true
One and one and one is two.

RESTING PLACE

They found him
in the living room
A nest comprised
of all his stuff
A faded card
gave up his name

Everyone deserves
a resting place
A resting place

They tried to find
a next of kin
No family ties
to be unbroken
They pawed the place
in rubber gloves

Everyone deserves
a reckoning
A reckoning

We enter as strangers
we hope to leave with friends
we enter as strangers
we hope to leave a print
of something more

He liked to hang out
at the bar
Identified by
his flannel

He liked to tell
silly jokes

Everyone deserves
a narrative
A narrative

He lies beneath
a willow tree
An overgrown
Potter's field
A name and date
mark the spot

Everyone deserves
remembering
Remembering

THE BREAK AWAY

Two hearts in love with each other
They're pacing about the floor
One thought in mind but neither one knows for sure
Each time they look at each other
They smile and then turn away
Which night? Which one?
Who led them to feel this way?

> "I've done you wrong - I can't hold on
> Feeling you've done the same."

Two hearts in love with each other
Both making their mental notes
Be home by six but make that little detour first
She thinks he'll be too busy to notice
He thinks that she will never know
And with regret they carry their hearts in tow

> "I still love you - but I've been untrue
> We've got to break away."

Two hearts not in love with each other
But not wanting the other to hurt
Suspicions rise as well as their feelings of guilt
They think that they can live with each other
But they can't even live with themselves
It's no surprise they're putting each other through hell

> They're digging inside their hearts
> And always coming up empty
> They're pulling each other apart for you - and me.

SOMETHING

Fade
and forget your troubles

Sit
and be thankful

Something that's often left unsaid
fools try to walk in angel's tread

Come
and embrace the quiet

Let
your mind wander

Something that's often left instead
we are easily misled

GET OVER

it's all a gift
a truce unspoken
we make the most
a tiny token

the petty and spite
is for posers
let in the light
it takes over

a song about time
gets fixed in the moment
10 years fly by
the cells in motion

to set in cement
and be frozen
is wasting too much
just get over
get over
get over

I'd be adrift
without my strong ties
they keep me tall
They are my allies

I normally veer
to the dark side
I cleaned up my act
and it's worldwide

this song's about hope
the real thing this time
the first I ever wrote
I find it sublime

to set in cement
and be frozen
is wasting too much
just get over
get over

ROUNDABOUT

it feels like
i've been here before
the signal mixed
bad semaphore
the fear guides us all
let's build up a wall
it worked so well before

it ain't no big
mystery
winners write
the history
we're on a losing path
bombs in the soundtrack
the war goes round and round

we go around around around
around around the roundabout

we go around around around
around around the roundabout

we go around around around
around around the roundabout

we go around around around
around around around

i'm feeling mighty sick
'bout all this forced politick
orange-faced megaphone
revs up mindless clones
the hate is getting hot

it's good they don't
teach this stuff in school
next hitler'll seem brand new
i'm filled with doublespeak
put there by thought police
the lie goes round and round

    we go around around around
    around around the roundabout

    we go around around around
    around around the roundabout

    we go around around around
    around around the roundabout

    we go around around around
    around around around

BREAD AND CIRCUSES

I like pretty pictures
on the screen
I like knowing
the latest meme
I feel incomplete
but I'll fill it, distill it

I like sharing
the latest news
It reinforces my worldview
I shout profanity
in the street, so discrete

Give me bread and circuses
Give me bread and circuses
Divert my eyes from the spark
Mesmerize it's a hidden art
Give me bread and circuses

I see wild fictions
on the screen
polished high
to show the sheen
Gather sand
for the Colesseum
hunger peaks, race is sweet

The barker calls
from the carnival
The game soon
turns to bloody brawl
We applaud on our feet
rinse and repeat, repeat

Give me bread and circuses
Give me bread and circuses
Divert my eyes from the spark
Mesmerize it's a hidden art
Give me bread and circuses

The BEIGE
2018

GASLIGHT

The fumes
Permeate the air
Cut through
Your mocking glare
The lights dim
Table starts to shake

You can't believe
What you read and see
You pound this thought
Deep into me
It starts to set
Baker's tray is full

And there's something off in the universe
Something off in the universe
Gaslight

Take my hand
Lead me astray
Crackpot logic
Sold-out doomsday
I want to believe
In anything

All monsters
From far away lands
Convenient scapegoats
Hide devious plans
They're not the threat
It's your small idle hands

And there's something off in the universe
Something off in the universe
Gaslight

Wake now
From this fever dream
Tempest tweets
Take down this fiend
Restore the light
The ship back on course

And there's something off in the universe
Something off in the universe
Gaslight

OUTLIER

I was once a princess
Sitting on a bus
Captive to madam's jeers
"You're not one of us."

I was once a sailor
Unsteady on my feet
Couldn't play the reindeer games
Too easy to beat

My side
Is outside
A view at least
It's not easy

I was once a dancer
Bending at my knees
Try to hide my face from the crowd
I dance just for me

I am still that princess
My home is my crown
It's where I go to figure things out
Without all the sound

My side
Is outside
A view at least
It's not easy

My side
Is outside
A view at least
It's never easy

MAGICAL THINKING

Sometimes I wish
On a traffic light

If I make it through red
I'll be all right

It's my magical thinking
It sometimes stops me from drinking

But usually not
Usually not

It's like getting up
On a Monday morning

I take the sunlight
On my face as a warning

Sometimes I am proven wrong
Because things aren't so bad after all

But usually not
Usually not

Whatever happened to
positive thinking?

Whatever happened to
positive thinking?

Whatever happened to
positive thinking?

Whatever happened to
Whatever happened to

I flip a coin
Into an empty fountain

I make a wish
That I won't be forgotten

Sometimes I look
For recognition

Before I switch
On the ignition

But usually not
Usually not
Usually not.

ADVENTURER

She's an adventurer I hate to say it
And I'm a ball and chain around her ankle

And when I'm waiting to be let out on bail
She'll be dreaming of her next island to sail to

My baby's gone away

She's a cosmonaut charting her next course
And there's no room for me on this mission, of course

And there is nothing I could do or say
that would ever make her want to stay here.

My baby's gone away

She's aiming high
I'm sinking low
She is in the sky
And I'm in a hole

I got a letter from Anchorage, Alaska today
It's warmer than she had imagined in the month of May
She said, "I'll miss you a lot, but that's OK
Because I'm leaving for Hong Kong in another day."

My baby's gone away
My baby's gone away

"So long!"

CRUEL WILL

you can't control
the monster that you've become
but i can choose
to stay away forever
so i do, i do

you broke apart
the pieces scattered everywhere
i can't keep up
with the blankness of your stare
your stare

the cruel fate
the world has handed us
we fight until
we die

you never knew
that i could see through you
a coat of paint can't
cover up those scars, those scars

you mistook
my question for interest
i don't care what happens
at the end of this road
this road

the cruel fate
the world has handed us
we fight until
we die

the status quo
is mayhem and misery
you'll never grow
beyond this illusion of purpose
purpose

your face is dull
free of expression
a clean sweep
of angry depression underneath
underneath

the cruel fate
the world has handed us
we fight until
we die

the free will
you calmly threw away
makes you fight
until...

AROUND THESE PARTS

around these parts
people feeling mighty low
mighty low
it's getting cold
and the factory is shutting down

we forget our part in it all
we turn our backs on the past

around these parts
the blame takes up space
takes up space
someone's lying and
someone is paying more

we forget we are strong
they pit us against ourselves

that's how the story goes
we turn against
all we know
that's how the story goes

around these parts
people hoping for some luck
for some luck
they scratch off tickets
tuck money in their socks

All the riches in the world
in the hands of so few

around these parts
people trying to stay alive
algorithms log rhythms
with the odds
we must choose how we live
we should choose not to die

that's how the story goes
we turn against
all we know
that's how the story goes

SOME THINGS

It must have been
The wrong place, the wrong time
To make it look like it was you
Who committed a crime
Should you testify as years go by,
And you have your day
And wonder if justice is just any way

Some things are better left unsaid
To those who know that they misled
Some ties need to be undone
To know what is right, and what is wrong

You saw it from the right angle
From the right side
To bear witness to the fact
Can you believe your eyes?
Should you stay quiet like all the rest,
Or let truth be the test?
Lies never make the better best.

A picture's worth a thousand words
When justice is finally served
Some trials are hell on earth
And this you know you don't deserve

The judge asked the jury
What they had found
You held your breath, so to hear
What was handed down
The foreman spoke complete and said,
"A verdict has been reached

Not guilty of the crime...
You are free!"

Sometimes you have to shout aloud
For those who haven't figured out
How to stand up and to fight for–
For all the rights we had before.

SHROUD

A click
for a witness
A smile
at a distance

Alone in a crowd
Your own little shroud
Covers you
Covers you

A poke
in passing
A joke
no one's laughing

Alone in a crowd
Your own little shroud

A stage of games
awaits you
Play the part
that breaks you
Mark the spot
Build up that plot
That's all that's left for you

A fear
of spaces
A shift
in phases

Alone in a crowd
Your own little shroud
Covers you
Covers you

A lie
worth telling
Is more
compelling

Alone in a crowd
Your own little shroud

A stage of games
awaits you
Play the part
that breaks you
Mark the spot
Build up that plot
That's all that's left for you

REGRET

I'm what you'll regret
If I take the step back
Behind the swingin' door
To the one I once adored

Oh, no it's not clear
How I got in here
No, oh it's not safe
Running out of space

You cut me out with ease
Me and my disease
Now I'm not so tall
I'm forever falling

Fall beneath the sky
My eyes won't deny
The walls I kept in place
Left me without you

I'm what you'll regret
Please don't take me back
I'm what you'll regret
Please don't take me back
I'm what you'll regret

SAVIOR

cowed and afraid
by strange sounds
and bright lights
that never will dim

we shift along
on an aimless path
feeling certain
that we'll never win

you'll never know
who you really are
till your faced with
the worst of defeat
and you sink
you sink

we all crave a savior
we all crave a savior
someone who'll show
us the sun in his pocket
someone who'll mark
the x for the gold
though where he leads us
is twisted and ugly
and broken
and full up in rage
full up in rage

never believe
anyone who says
he knows
how to make it
great again

there's no quick fix
no a to z
that will cure
the malaise
within

still we seek it
the cure all
that will deliver
hope
that deflates
conflates

we all crave a stranger
we all crave a stranger
someone who'll take our
heart and unlock it
someone who sees
what no one else does
though it's an illusion
that's blurry
unfocused and filmy
a mirror

we all crave
we all crave
we all crave

someone to lighten the load
someone to break the mold
but ambition breeds weakness
our heroes are few
so watch how the villains prevail

Sleeping World
2019

BIG WHITE LIE

Gonna put it in your pocket
And there's no need to lock it
Can I tell you a secret
And not care if you keep it.

We're all livin' in a big white lie
We're all livin' in a big white lie
We're all livin' in a big white lie

I am standing on the floor
I am staring at the door
I am pushing for some more
And my arm is getting sore

We're all livin' in a big white lie
We're all livin' in a big white lie
We're all livin' in a big white lie

If the story is not true / Say it isn't so
The protagonist is you / I think it's time to go
And the narrative is square / And I'm sinkin' low
The plot thread bare / Let's just end the show

We're all livin' in a big white lie
We're all livin' in a big white lie
We're all livin' in a big white lie

FANTASY

The day it grinds us to our core
Only to leave us wanting more

The years peel away our masks
Until we don't know what to ask

The first time I saw your face
It stunned me

This isn't you, this isn't me
But just a need for a fantasy

How did it ever come to this
Only to betray with a list

When did it really get so wrong
I didn't want to write this song

The last time I saw your face
It stunned me

It wasn't you, it wasn't me
It's just a need for a fantasy

COLLECTIVE DEMENTIA

We long for something else
Something that never was
Something we can't even define

We long for a connect
In a lion's cage
That will only leave us
Torn and frayed

Pride is the fall
Fragile decoy
Collective dementia

We shout into the void
About things we've never read
About things we've never seen

We settle on a foe
Solid as evening fog
So we don't have to deal
With what we've done

Pride is the fall
Fragile decoy
Collective dementia

XMAS IN JUNE

Exposing the bluff
The emperor in the buff
Tunics on the table
Now we're not so tough

Waterways and travel
Sheep amongst the cattle
The aqueducts receding
Now we're off to battle

Christmas in June
I never meant to hurt you
I never meant to make you cry
The Dalai Lama is not worried

There's two to play the game
Shame on top of shame
Screen test affidavit
Now we're all the same

Writing you a letter
The key inside a feather
Your career and your future
Never looking better

Christmas in June
I never meant to hurt you
I never meant to make you cry
The Dalai Lama is not worried

NUMB THE FALL

The ease with the world
I am throwing away
As I set my glass down

To face head on
Who we should really be
Is the biggest letdown

To numb the fall
Numb the fall

The bubbles rise
And I try to push back
It's too early
To deal with this now

We live next door
But act miles away
As we shutter
The liquid allows

To numb the fall
Numb the fall

The memory fades
Fuzzy and pink
I marvel
Marbles in mouth

Erudite wit
Repeating myself
I'm a legend
In my own mind

To numb the fall
Numb the fall

HOT SUMMER NIGHTS

Catch the UVs on the beach
Sand takes over our feet
as the plastic intertwines

Music fills up the air
the diseases of despair
are as natural as the tides

It's the hottest summer night
It's the hottest summer of your life

Party's in full swing
Fire eats at the trees as the ashes
They all fall down

Build a wall on all sides
the end's televised as the mercury
beats its rise

It's the hottest summer night
It's the hottest summer of your life

Don't you wanna get somewhere cooler
The air's hard to breathe over here
Don't you wanna go some place cooler
The land's disappearing everywhere

It's the hottest summer of your life

Catch a chunk as it breaks
a giant ice earthquake
fill the drinks that slip on by

Numb is how I'll go watching all the show
it's a masterpiece of our demise

It's the hottest summer night
It's the hottest summer of your life
It's the hottest summer
It's the hottest summer
It's the hottest summer
of your life

BLINDERS

Switch—turn the vent on full blast
Stop—let it hit head on
Cheer—for the games have just started
Run—but there's nowhere to go

When you go through life with blinders on
And you think that you're seeing the sun
And you jumped with the band
Forsaken the plan of love
You're done. You're done
You're done. You're done.

Choose—for there's always an option
Speak—for those without a song
Split—for you're made up of atoms
Like those who you drag through the mud

When you go through life with blinders on
And you think that you're seeing the sun
And you jumped with the band
Forsaken the plan of love
You're done.

This ain't the train you wanna be on
Empty signs forced paragons
Get off while the night's still young
And you'll be fine no faux divine

False—that's the name for the prophet
Fake—are the promises kept
Lose—that's what we're all doing
Weep—for the nation that slept
When you go through life with blinders on

TO BE A WOMAN

I get paid less for the same work
I'm told to smile by every single jerk

It's fun to be a woman

I get catcalls walking down the street
from all these folks I'd never want to meet.

It's fun to be a woman
Oh, it's fun to be a woman

They pass these laws that make it hard to be
They rule my uterus like it's their property

It's fun to be a woman

They say be glad you don't live in Iran
Well, our mullahs are covered in spray tan

It's fun to be a woman
Oh, it's fun to be a woman

We can't even get our ERA
"But her emails!" is what they say

I'm supposed to wear a size 2
And be younger and sexy
And not say, "No," to you

It's fun to be a woman

I hear there's a thing called legitimate rape
Like all that other stuff is merely knee scrapes

It's fun to be a woman
Oh, it's fun to be a woman

This song might piss you off
but I don't really care
You got your judge
Who really likes his beer.

It's fun to be a woman
Oh, it's fun to be a woman
One more time
It's fun to be a woman

DON'T FORGET

You wouldn't have shown up
If I didn't call
If you didn't care
You wouldn't have come
To the same place where we used to live

We know it's over
We know it's through
The games we played
Were always up to you

Could you give this dead man
One last request?

Don't forget the good times
Please forgive the bad

One more night
One more night
One more night

And I know, he's got a brand new car
I still got a broken heart
You hang around the snobby crowd
Laughing at this poor clown

Tomorrow is your wedding day
You still have a choice so please stay
Before you make your biggest mistake

Imagine you walking down the aisle
With a white dress and a sincere smile
For some reason
The picture don't fit the frame

Don't forget the good times
Please forgive the bad

One more night
One more night
One more night

WALKAWAY

You used to run away
From all your problems
I never could keep up with you
You used to run and hide
From all the others
"Hello, cruel world, how are you?"

And you know how I tried
To make us free
From the rattling chains that be.
Now I see you in a different light.
Lines on your face
Rings around your eyes

Let's walkaway
Walkaway from here

I used to be the oblivious one
Though you always were by my side
And when I jumped ship
I never called for help
I couldn't even if I tried

Then the rainy days
Began to fall on me
With no lifeboat in sight
Now you see me in a different light
Lines on my face
Rings around my eyes

Let's walkaway
Walkaway from here

Songs from the
Second Floor
2022

NO DETECTION

Call the roll for the new prinz
Takes a toll on the peasants
A neon sign, a poke in the eye
I repeat again and again

I walk the fields rest a bit
And huddle down in kinship
Take a hit for the home team
Just to hear the whole world sing

Eastward, westward
Any direction
Left, right, north, south
No detection

A pillow case, a civil suit
Above the fray, a hidden fruit
The book is done, story told
How profound it is

I sit around, await my orders
Is it a ploy, a kind of torture?
I take a call on the down low
Should I stay...or should I just disappear?

Topple down
Signs and symbols
I was witness
To *Murder the Word*

Eastward, westward
Any direction
Left, right, north, south
No detection

DECADES

Garden's covered in sand
There's no trees, there's no seedlings
As we make our demands
The whole world is retreating
Oh, the iron in our blood
Comes from the stars
Serves to show
How connected we are

If you say that it's so
It don't mean I believe it
We can't bridge the divide
There's no will to defeat it
As you quote from your book
And I quote from mine
Parallels are there
But hate is defined

Here's the start of a terribly wonderful decade
At the cusp of a wonderfully terrible decade

There is light in despair
There is joy in meaning
There are shrines to tear down
And some are worth keeping
As we sift through the ash
We can show who we are
Phoenix feathers
Cause all of the sparks

There is pain in truth
In fact lies are so easy
Take a bite of this fruit
It is time to see clearly
Oh, the countdown's begun
Koalas on the run
Precious sands
In the barrel of a gun

Here's the start of a terribly wonderful decade
At the cusp of a wonderfully terrible decade

HEADING NOWHERE AGAIN

Sun shinin' lazily on me
And I've just sailed through another endless day

Unwindin' in this paradise
Makes it hard to think of waking up tonight

Flying through the skies with the world in my eyes
...as I gaze out my window

No one knows but me
No one knows but me,
The shape I'm in, heading nowhere again

Through the haze I clearly see I'm surrounded
Trapped up like a thief on a silent movie screen

A vanishing act in the dead of night if I'm successful
'The stage is set for a final farewell scene

Flying through the skies with the world in my eyes
...as I gaze out my window

No one knows but me
No one knows but me,
The shape I'm in, heading nowhere again

END THE END

It's not worth going out
Something in the air
Tonight is the night
Resist despair

It's not worth staying in
Begin the Beguine
Isolation
To face what we've done

It may be novel,
But it's nothing new
Just a gift from me to you
Or a kiss, after the ball
To regret once and for all

Tempt me to give up
The door, it stays shut
Before the law
When no one called

Oh, *Tumbling Dice!*
Wouldn't It Be Nice
To give *chance* a chance
For our last dance

It may be novel,
But it's nothing new
Just a gift from me to you
Or a kiss, after the fall
To regret once and for all

IT'S YOUR BIRTHDAY

It's your birthday
It's your birthday
So for today,
Do what you may

Today's the day
You get your way
So for today,
Do what you may

Your friends are here
But who knows where
They'll be another day

It's sunny now
But who knows how
To keep the clouds away

It's your birthday
It's your birthday
So for today,
Do what you may

Tomorrow comes
Your cake is done
So for today,
Do what you may

The candles lit
A throne to sit
And blow out
All of the lights

A knife to cut
A wish for luck
Before it turns to night

It's your birthday
It's your birthday
So for today,
Do what you may

Tomorrow comes
Your cake is gone
So for today,
Do what you may

ASTROLOGICAL SIGNS

I'm watching a man explode into rage
And wonder how he can think
He's exploited, he's entitled to it
He speaks in tongues, slimy freedoms
Are dripping and piling up on the floor,
Haunts to explore

I see you nanoseconds behind
Your past is my present
We're all siloed, invisibly tied
All headed toward descent

We can look at the sky
Our astrological signs
Are pointing down, down

Another day, another sign
That no one is getting
Out of this alive, out of this alive
Talking heads assigning blame
Pinned on top of a pile of sand
No one takes a stand

I see you standing alone
A shroud upon your head
We are linked self replicating
Drinks poured out to the dead

We can look at the sky
Our astrological signs
Are pointing down, down

Hunker down and settle in
The math in here is all division
Remainder is a sin
Astroturf can't silence the din
My chance card says I'll never win
Compromise is still

I see you falling behind
The past that never was
Nostalgia grips the seats
In the back, plant memory transcends

We can look at the sky
Our astrological signs
Are pointing down, down, down

RED LINE

The phonograph
has stopped its spinning
its last gasp
we swallow down
the bright prescription
of secrets past

We shove aside
inconvenience to
its bitter end
of this stand

We redefine the narrative
when we can't clap
our heroes aren't what they seem
and the story snaps

We reach for lies to deny
that it is us who's trapped
in this stand

And the crowd is at the gate
they're stomping and they're pounding
minds consumed by hate
that they can't see the time
it twists it serpentines
we've crossed that red line

They changed the hat
but not the message - a salute
to those who sketched
out the playbook
the grand pursuit

They wave some flags
of tired thread
and spill out all the grain
of this stand

We're not suppose to fight
the battles of the past
but those who say
you don't belong here
are growing fast

They'll rip apart
the very pieces
that barely fit in place
in this land

And the mob is at the gate
their mouths are fully frothing
throwing all the weight
of heavy troubled lies
fed and televised
we've crossed that red line

That they can't see the time
it twists it serpentines
we've crossed that red line

It's not the conversation
we're equipped to have

HOLIDAY IN AMERIKA

Death squads on the streets of Portland
Death squads on the streets of New York
Death squads on the streets of Austin
Death squads on the streets of Detroit

So you say you want a revolution
You better act before they get to you
Faceless agents are running down
Friends and family in your hometown

Calling all sisters and brothers
Only cowards tear gas mothers
Unmarked cars driving down main street
Did you hear that, could you feel the heat?

It's a clamp down if I've ever seen one
Your hypocrisy is drenched in treason
You swore an oath to the Constitution
And broke it for a final solution

Death squads on the streets of Philly
Death squads on the streets of LA
Death squads on the streets of Boston
Death squads gonna take your rights away

You think that this is law and order
When we can't even cross our own borders
Wake up before it's too late
This can't be the USA

HYPER INDIVIDUAL

When you stand outside yourself
You get a better view
And the pieces snap in place
Expands in grace
There are no islands
More an archipelago
That connect by filaments
Keep us afloat

You're a hyper individual
Only thinking 'bout yourself
You hyper individuals
While we burn burn burn
While it burns burns burns

There's a gulf that's widening
Unraveling history
A crack in common ground
Tectonic canyon

You worship idols
Made from paper and need
A servile sophist
Whose tongue gleams sweet

You're a hyper individual
Only thinking 'bout yourself
You hyper individuals
While we burn burn burn
While it burns burns burns

It's a made-up battle
With no end in sight
And the fuel is grievance
And petty slights
The mortal coil frays
The network gasps
And the stars ignite
Endless night

You're a hyper individual
Only thinking 'bout yourself
You hyper individuals
While we burn burn burn
While it burns burns burns

www.ingramcontent.com/pod-product-compliance
Lightning Source LLC
Chambersburg PA
CBHW072045160426
43197CB00014B/2637